American Colonial Furniture
in Scaled Drawings

Alvan Crocker Nye

Dover Publications, Inc.
New York

Published in Canada by General Publishing Company,
Ltd., 30 Lesmill Road, Don Mills, Toronto, Ontario.
Published in the United Kingdom by Constable and Company, Ltd.

This Dover edition, first published in 1982, is an unabridged republication of the work originally published in 1895 by William Helburn, New York, under the title *A Collection of Scale-drawings, Details, and Sketches of what is commonly known as Colonial Furniture, Measured and drawn from antique examples by Alvan Crocker Nye, Architect.*

Manufactured in the United States of America
Dover Publications, Inc.
180 Varick Street
New York, N.Y. 10014

Library of Congress Cataloging in Publication Data

Nye, Alvan Crocker.
    American colonial furniture in measured drawings.

    Reprint. Originally published: A collection of scale-drawings, details, and sketches of what is commonly known as colonial furniture. New York: W. Helburn, 1895.
    1. Furniture—Drawings. 2. Furniture, Colonial—United States. 3. Furniture, Early American.
    I. Title
TT196.N93   1982   749.213'022'3   82-7306
ISBN 0-486-21560-1 (pbk.)   AACR2

PREFACE.

THE following fifty-five sheets of drawings are part of a collection of measurements that were made for the purpose of becoming familiar with the details and proportions of the furniture of the 17th, 18th and early 19th centuries in this country.

To render them more useful they were carefully drawn to scale, and friends having expressed a desire of sharing the information thus obtained this much is now placed within reach.

No claims for anything more than a collection of drawings are made and consequently no text has been written. It will be observed that in the majority of instances where perspective sketches are given they are in the lower left-hand corner of the page. When so placed they have been constructed mechanically at a uniform scale; the angle to the picture plane and the point of sight being the same in all. When the perspective is not so placed it has not been constructed, but was sketched directly from the object.

No attempt has been made to give the age or a record of the articles illustrated, as, for several reasons, it seemed impracticable.

On the under side of the seat of the chair shown on plate seventeen there was written with ink on the webbing this inscription: "Sam Davies, Upholsterer, Newbury St., Boston, July 1791."

The arm chair shown on plate ten also has 1623 painted on it, as the date when the chair came into the possession of the antecedents of the family now owning it.

An effort was made to learn the history of the couch (plate twenty-six) but nothing was known beyond that it had been in the family about two hundred and thirty years.

Credit can not be given here to all who have aided me in this task.

When the articles measured are owned by societies they are credited with them on the drawing itself.

I particularly express my thanks to them, and to the individuals who have allowed me to enter their homes to study their treasured antiquities.

To those who have secured introductions or furnished information I also acknowledge my obligations.

It is hoped that what is herewith sent forth will prove as serviceable and entertaining to others as it has been to me.

ALVAN CROCKER NYE

October 1895, NEW YORK CITY.

THE TOP OF A MIRROR.

PAINTED ON AN OLD CHEST. MEMORIAL HALL. DEERFIELD, MASS.

CONTENTS.

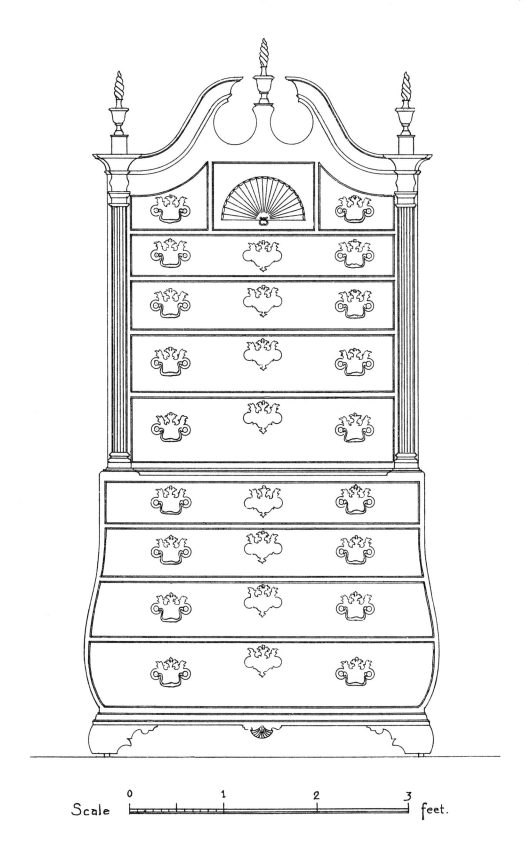

Scale   0   1   2   3   feet.

Side Elevation and Details
of the chest of drawers
shown on sheet number ①

Ⓐ

Plan through pilaster.

Ⓑ   Ⓒ

Ⓐ

Ⓑ

Ⓒ

0   1   2   3
Scale   inches

0   1   2   3
Scale   feet

High-boy.
Cheſt of drawers.

Finials are
missing⸮

Scale   0   1   2   3   feet.

High-boy.

Cheſt of drawers.

Plan of leg   x   ½ Plan.

Scale   0   1   2   3   feet

Turned Finials.

Taken from "High-boys."

Square

Square

Square

Scale |———|———|———|———| inches.

0   1   2   3   4

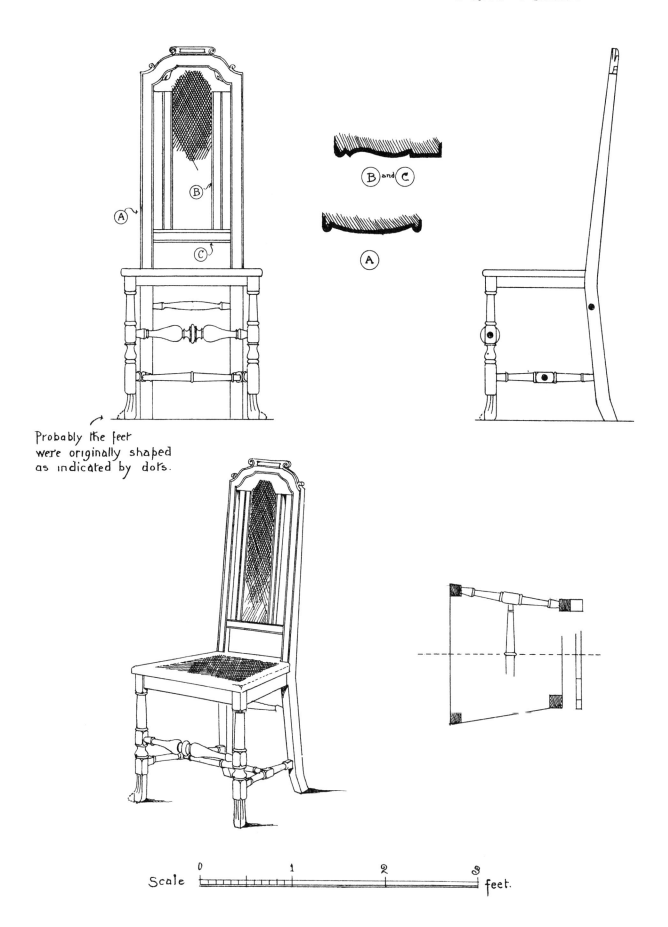

Probably the feet
were originally shaped
as indicated by dots.

Scale   0   1   2   3   feet.

Cane Chair ⑦

In the rooms of The American Antiquarian Society,
Worcester, Mass.

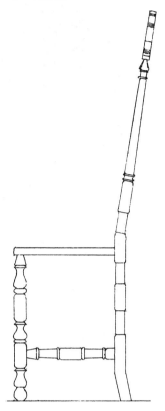

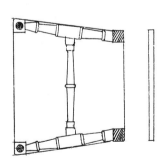

Scale  feet.

Cane Chairs.

A

Foot restored.

Foot as it exists

B

Scale 0 1 2 3 feet.

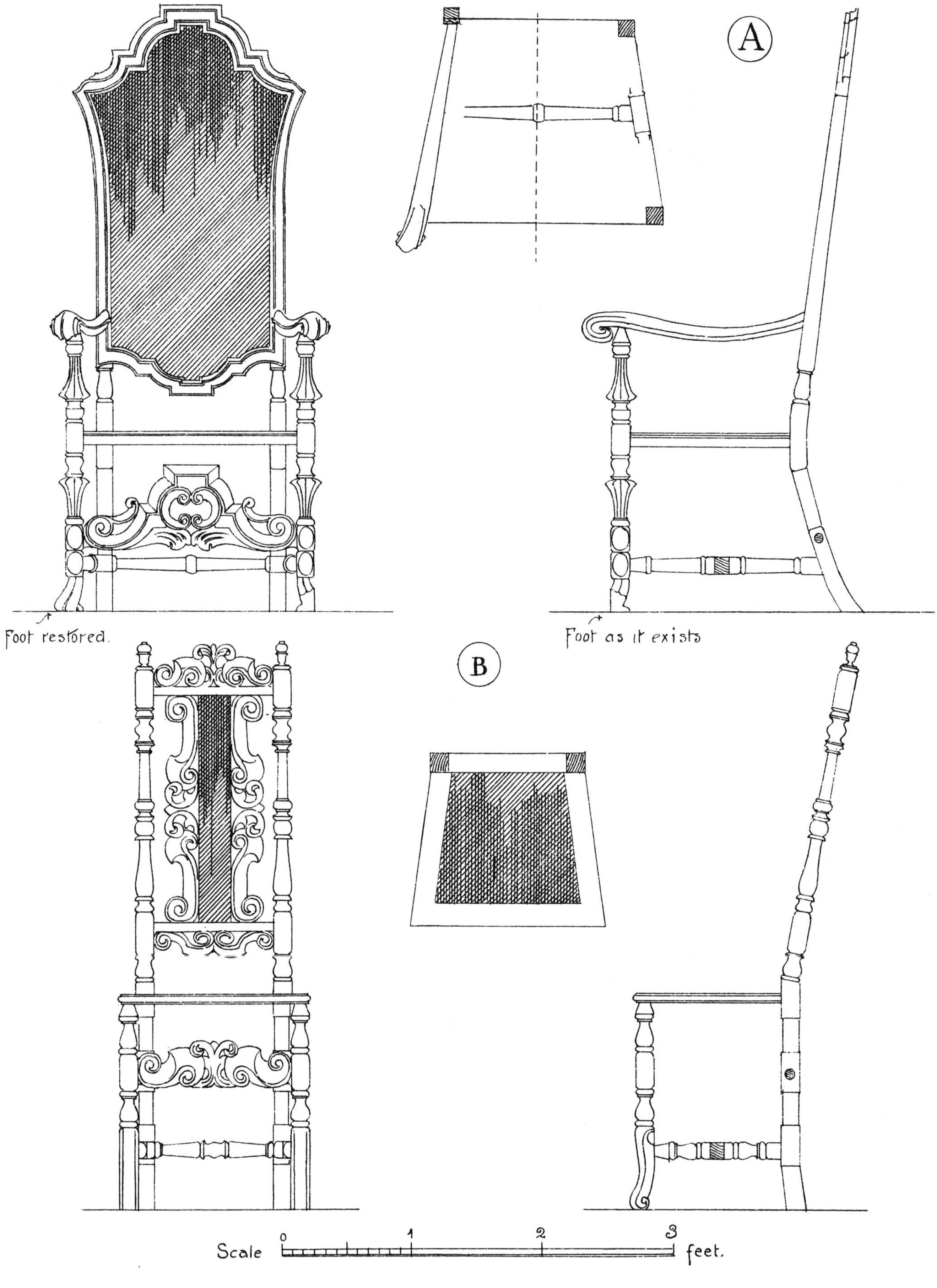

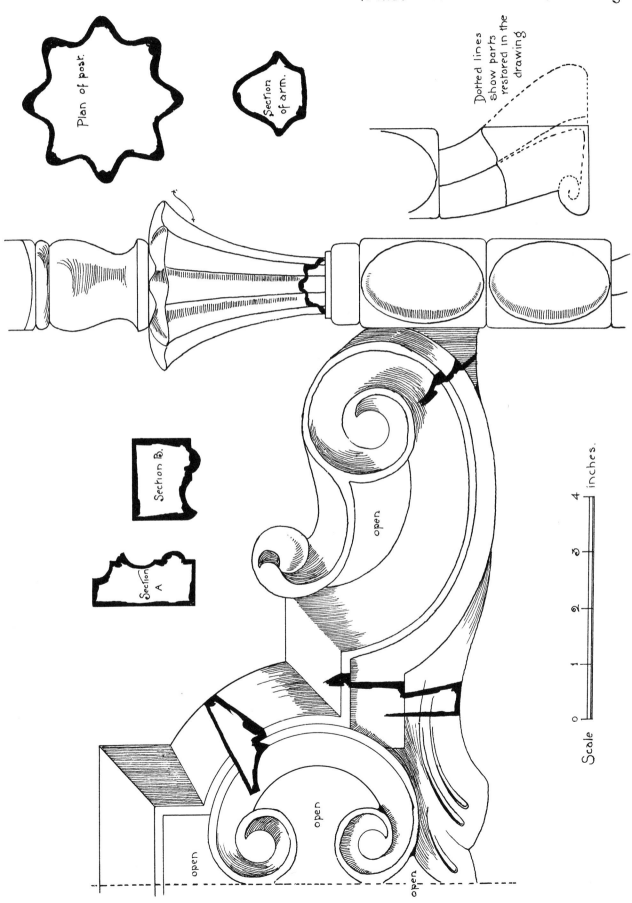

Detail of Chair "A"
shown on sheet number (8).
To illustrate character of carving.

Plan of post.

Section of arm.

Dotted lines show parts restored in the drawing

Section B.

Section A.

open

open

open

open

Scale

0 1 2 3 4 inches.

Bannister Backed Chairs.

Bannisters of the back are half turnings with the flat side set toward the front.

The chair without arms is in the rooms of the Connecticut Historical Society, Hartford, Conn.

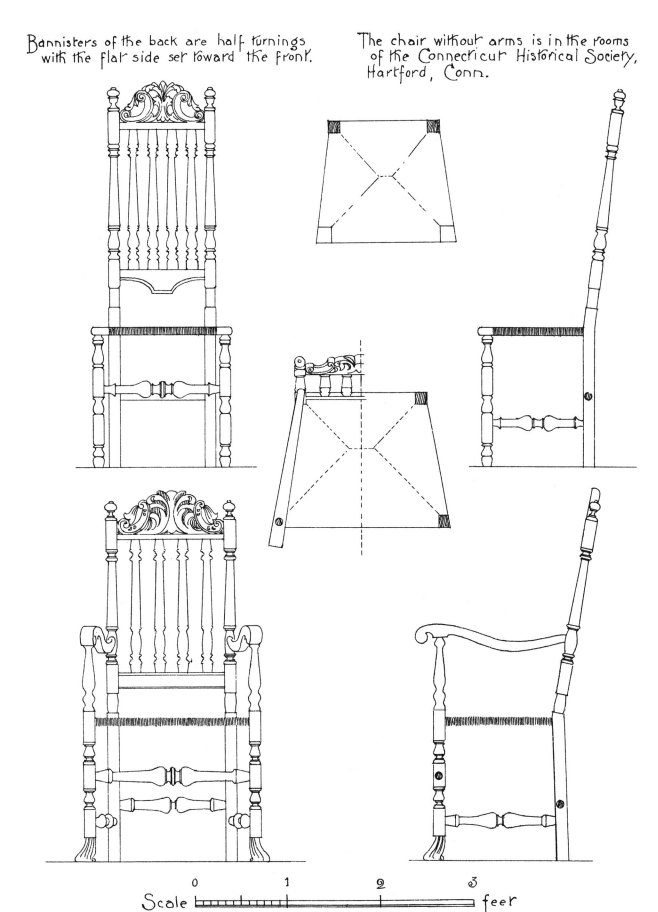

Scale |⊢⊢⊢⊢⊢⊢⊢⊢⊢⊢⊢⊢| feet

0   1   2   3

Back

Back

Front Stretcher.

Back of Nº ⑥

Back of Nº ⑦

Front Stretcher Nº ⑦

Back of Nº ⑧ B

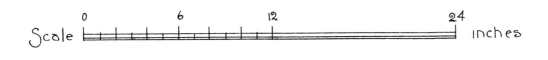

Scale 0 6 12 24 inches

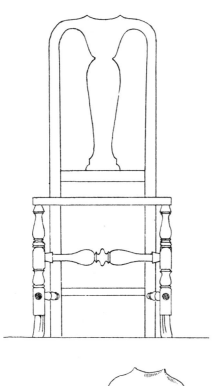

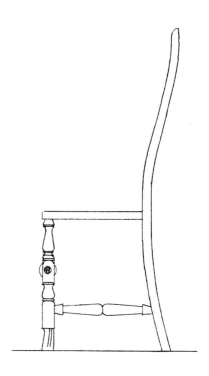

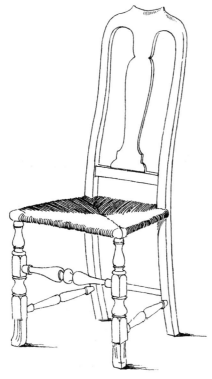

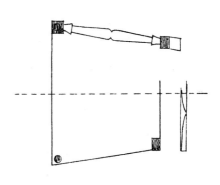

Scale   0   1   2   3 feet.

High backed Leather Chair.

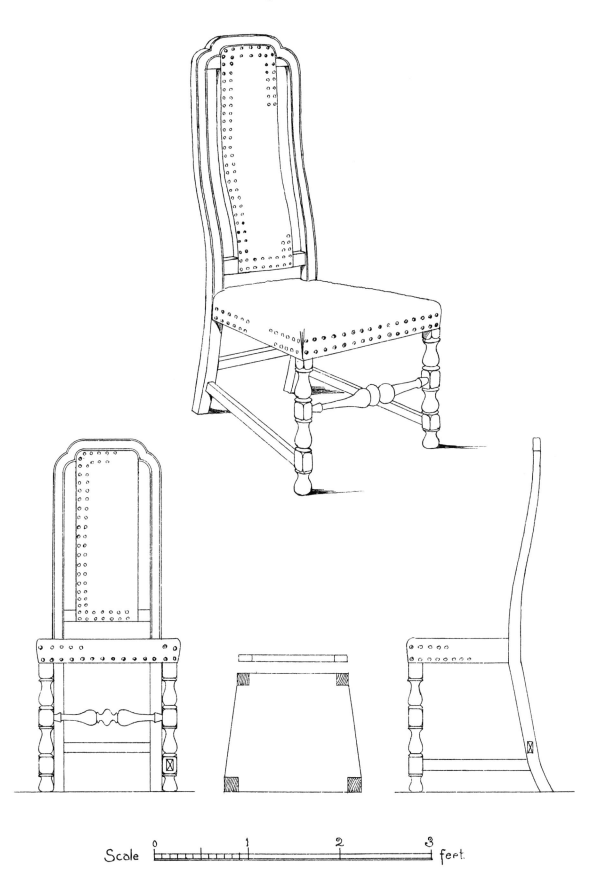

Scale   0   1   2   3   feet.

Leather Chair

In Memorial Hall.
Deerfield, Mass.

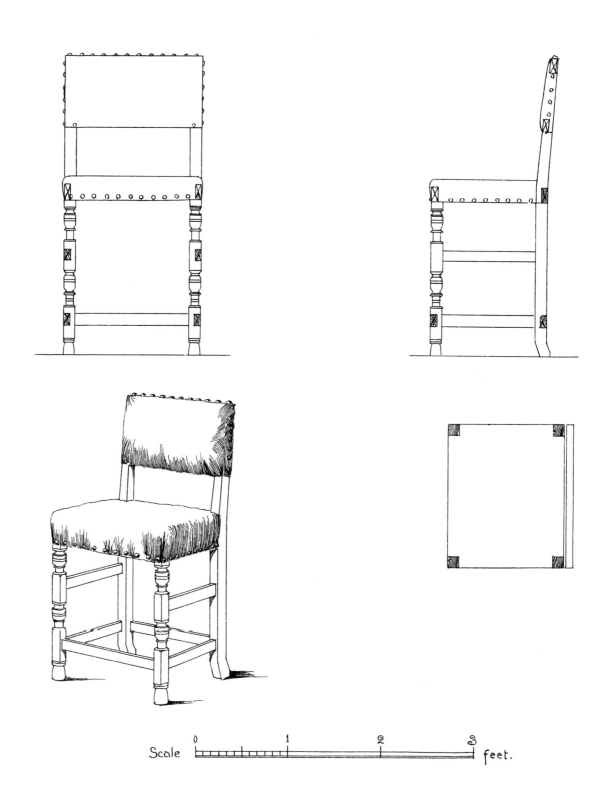

Scale 0   1   2   3 feet.

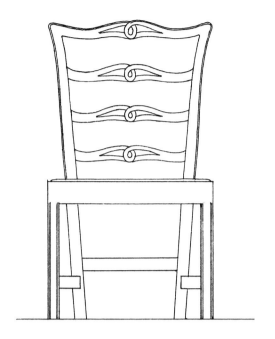

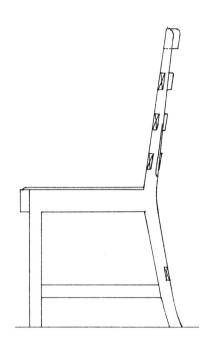

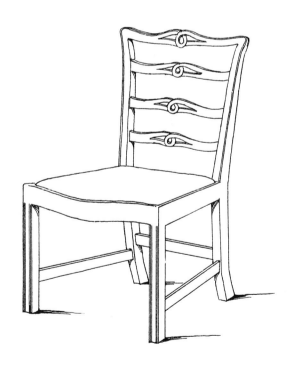

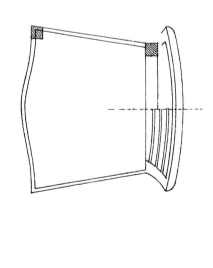

Scale ⓪ ⓵ ⓶ ⓷ feet.

Chair.

In the rooms of The American Antiquarian Society,
Worcester, Mass.

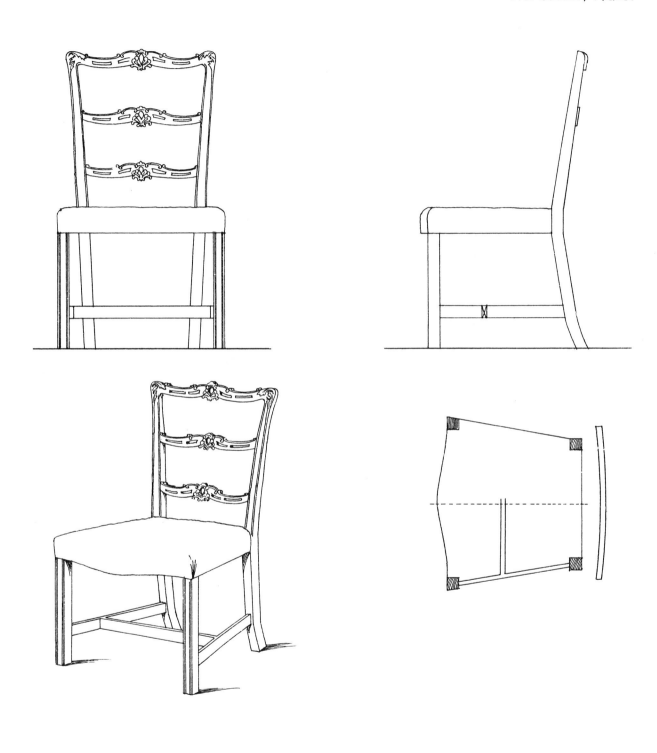

Scale ⊢⊢⊢⊢⊢⊢⊢⊢⊢⊣ feet.
0   1   2   3

Chair.
Heppelwhite pattern.

(17)

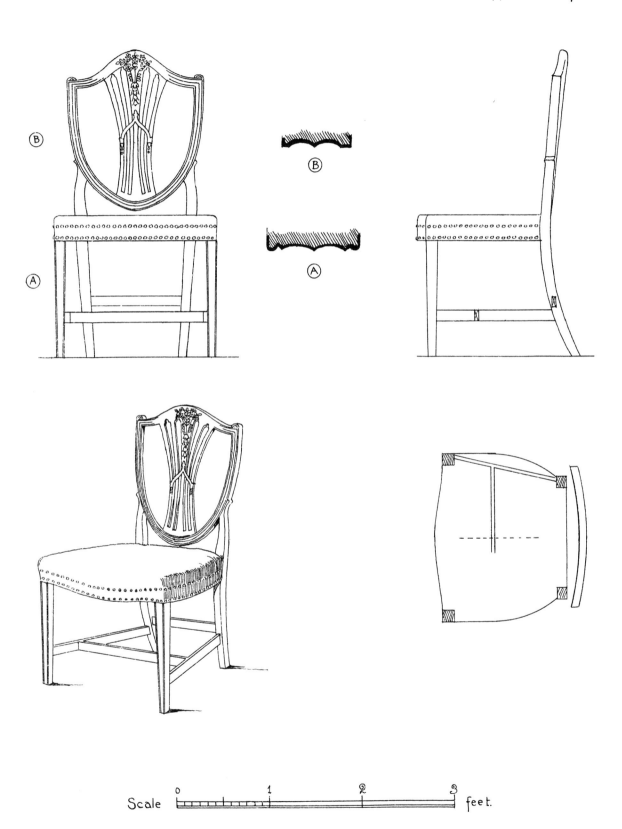

B

A

Scale 0   1   2   3 feet.

(A)

(B)

(C)

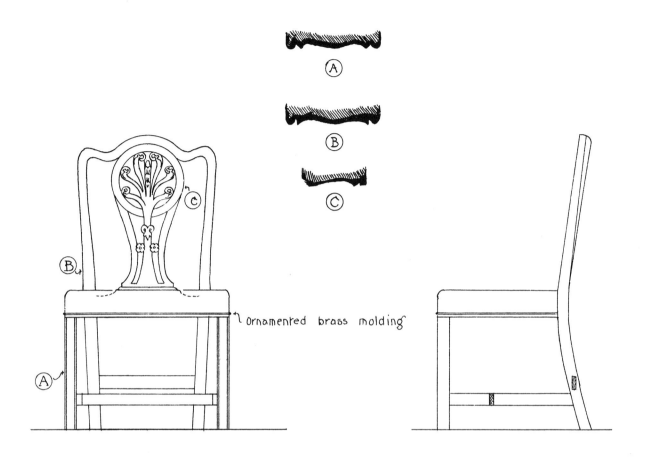

Ornamented brass molding

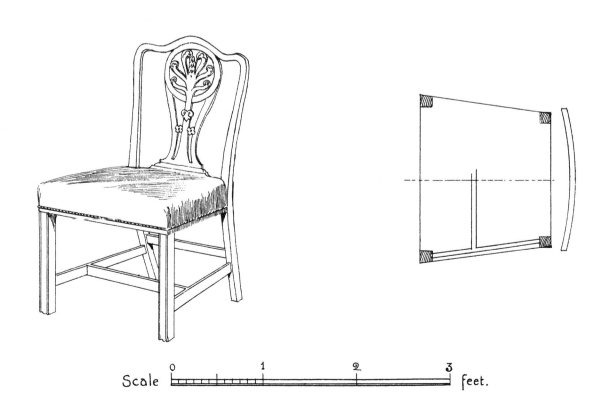

Scale 0 1 2 3 feet.

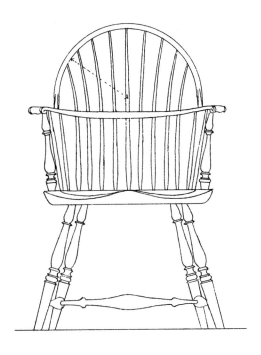

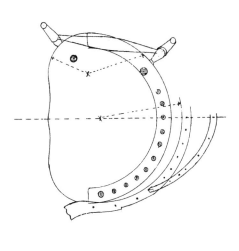

Scale 0 1 2 3 feet.

A Childs Turned Chair

In the rooms of The American Antiquarian Society.
Worcester, Mass.

Brought to this country by
Richard Mather, grandfather of
Cotton Mather, in 1635.

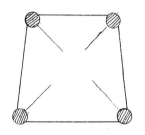

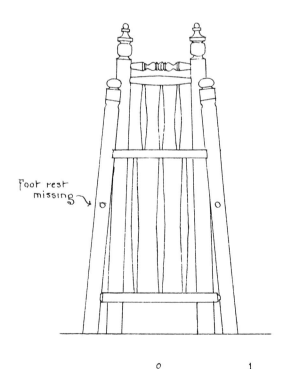

Foot rest
missing

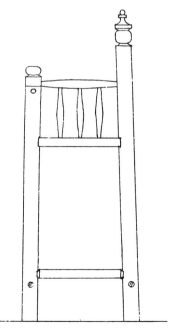

Scale
0   1   2   3
feet.

Roundabout Chair

In the Memorial Hall
Deerfield, Mass.

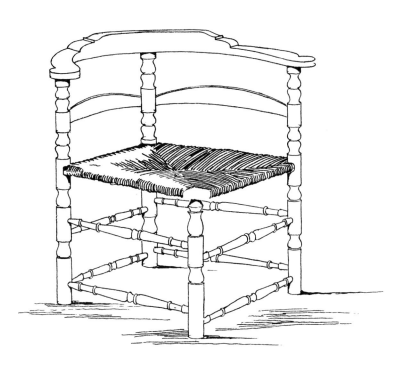

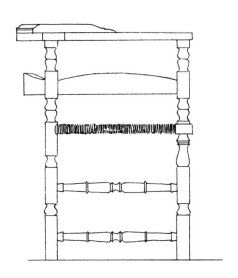

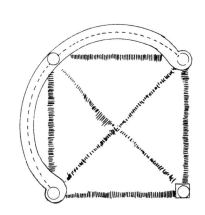

Scale

0   1   2   3   feet.

Roundabout Chair.

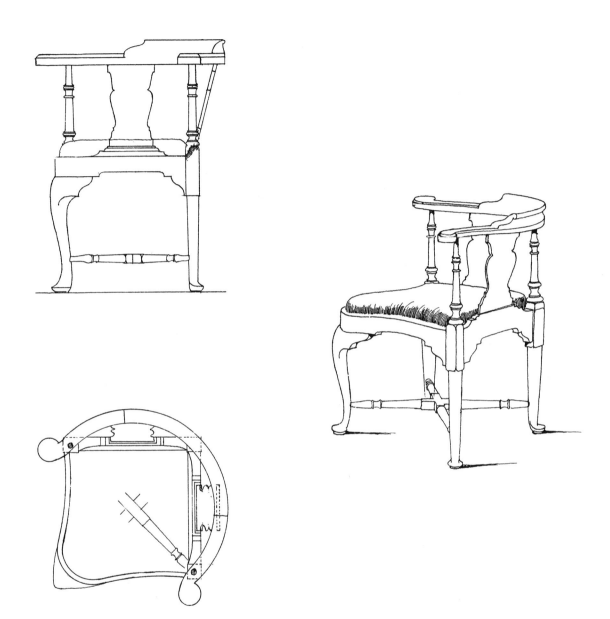

Scale  feet

0   1   2   3

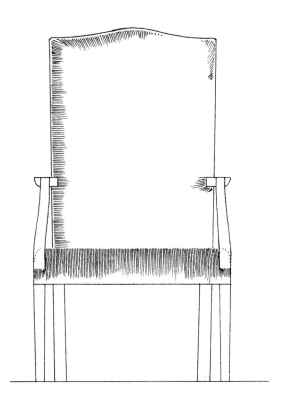

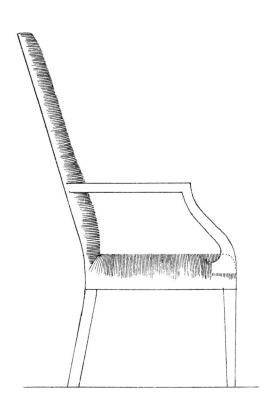

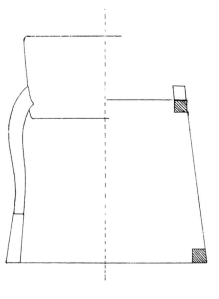

Easy Chair.

½ plan above · ½ plan below seat.

Scale   0   1   2   3   feet.

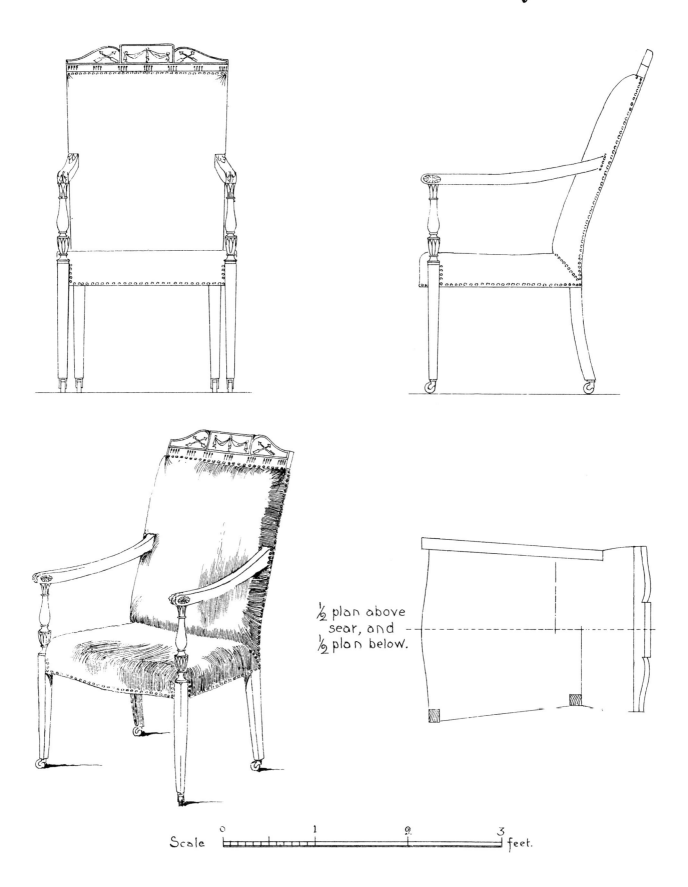

½ plan above
seat, and
½ plan below.

Scale 0   1   2   3 feet.

Easy Chair.

All upholstered

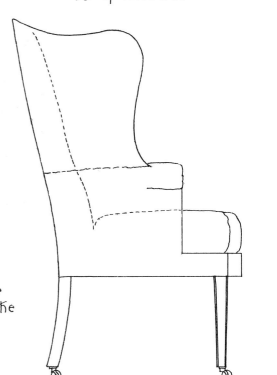

feather cushion

Flounce around the
seat is omitted on the
scale drawing.

½ Front elevation. × ½ back elevation.

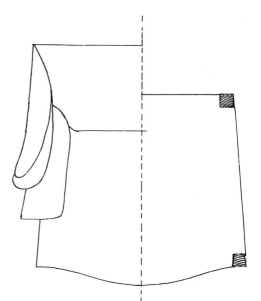

½ plan above × ½ plan below
the seat.

Scale |━━━━━━━━━━━━━━━━━━━━━━| feet.
0   1   2   3

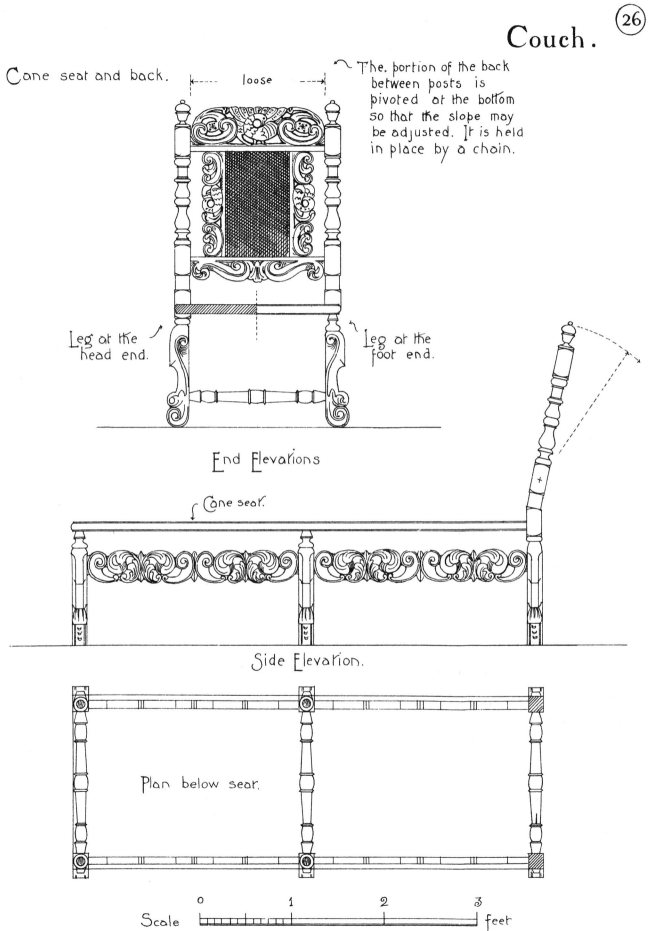

Couch. 26

Cane seat and back.

loose

~ The portion of the back between posts is pivoted at the bottom so that the slope may be adjusted. It is held in place by a chain.

Leg at the head end.

Leg at the foot end.

End Elevations

Cane seat.

Side Elevation.

Plan below seat.

Scale

0 1 2 3 feet

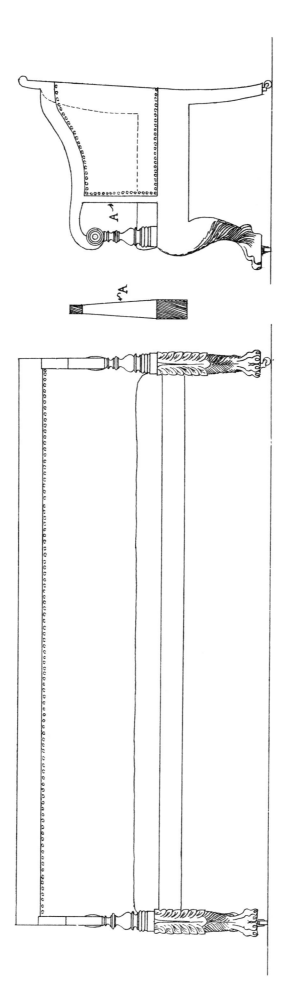

Scale

3 feet.

2

1

0

Sofa.

In the rooms of The American Antiquarian Society,
Worcester, Mass.

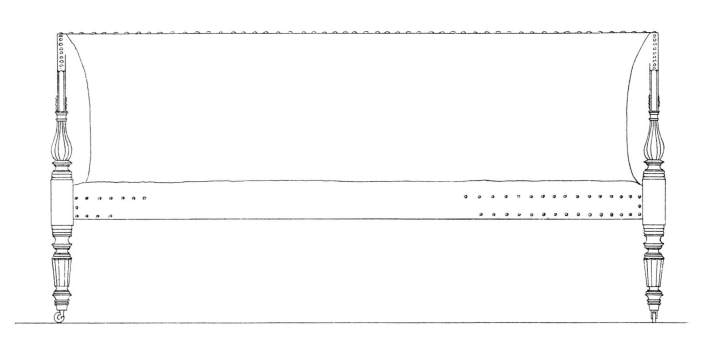

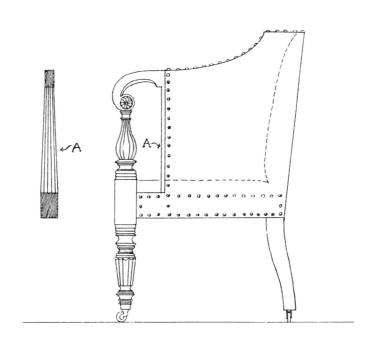

A

A

Scale 0 1 2 3 feet.

Sofa

In the rooms of The American Antiquarian Society,
Worcester, Mass.

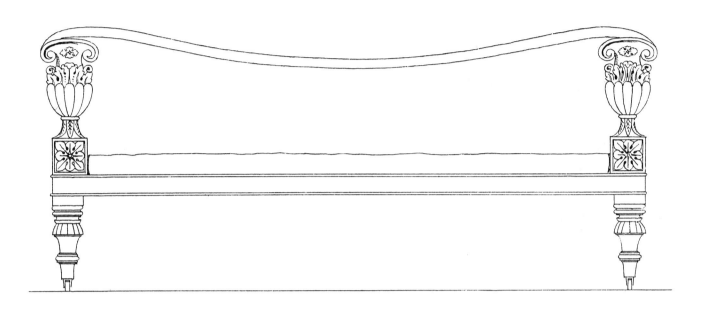

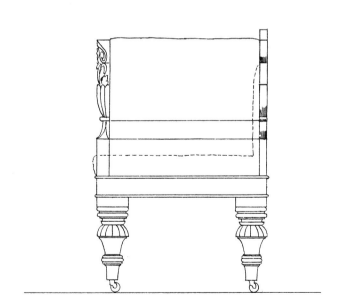

Scale  feet.

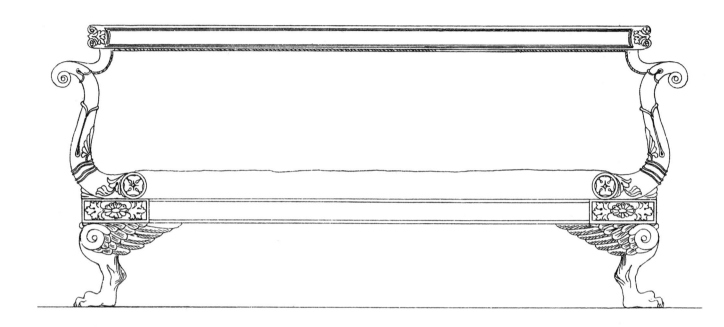

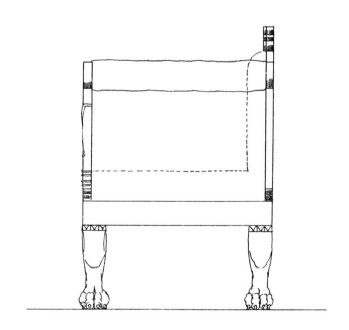

Scale |⊢⊢⊢⊢⊢⊢⊢⊢⊢⊢⊢⊢⊢⊢⊢⊢⊢⊢⊢⊢⊢⊢⊢⊢| feet.
      0   1   2   3

Sofa. ③¹

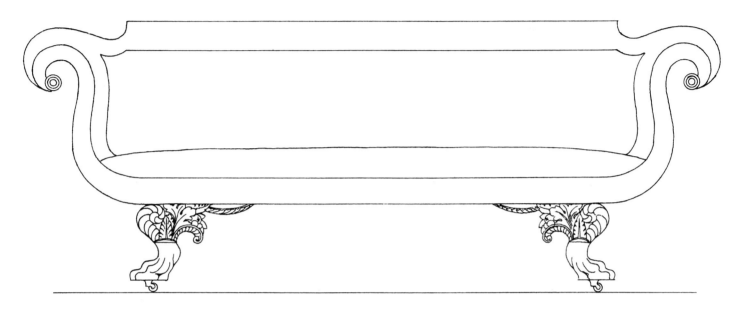

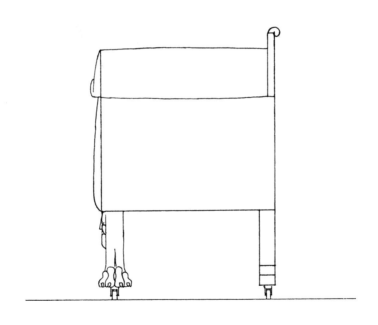

Scale  feet.

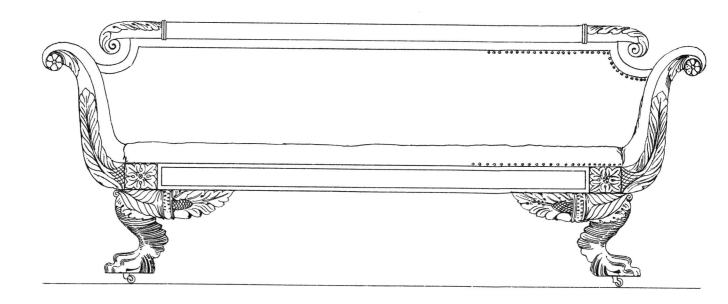

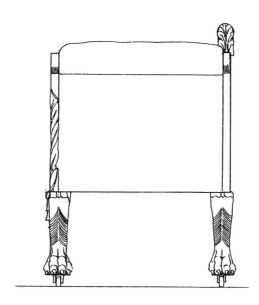

Scale 0   1   2   3 feet

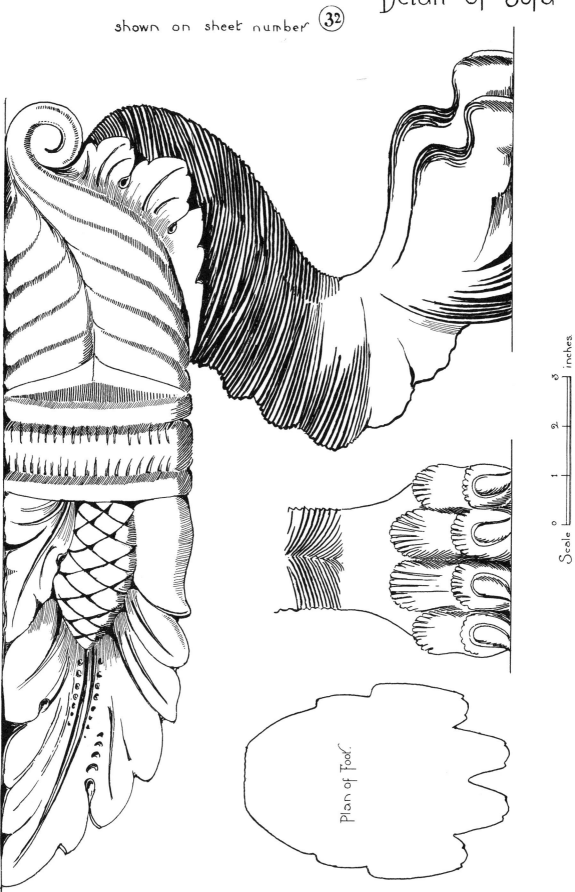

shown on sheet number ㉜

Scale 0 1 2 3 inches.

Plan of Foot.

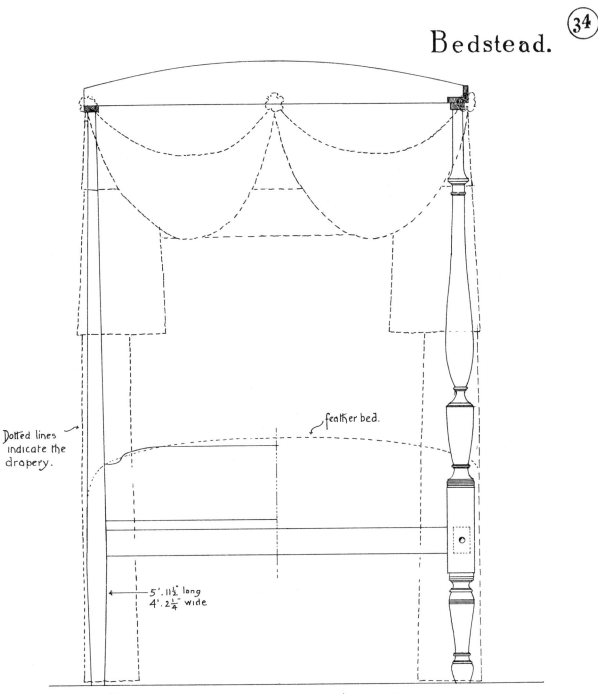

Dotted lines
indicate the
drapery.

feather bed.

5'. 11½" long
4'. 2¼" wide

Half elevation of head.

Half elevation of foot.

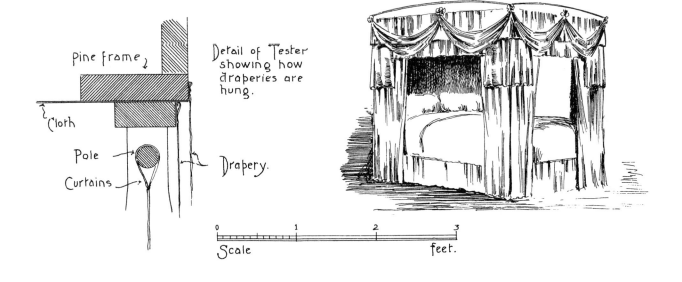

Pine frame

Cloth

Pole

Curtains

Detail of Tester
showing how
draperies are
hung.

Drapery.

0   1   2   3
Scale   feet.

Bedposts.

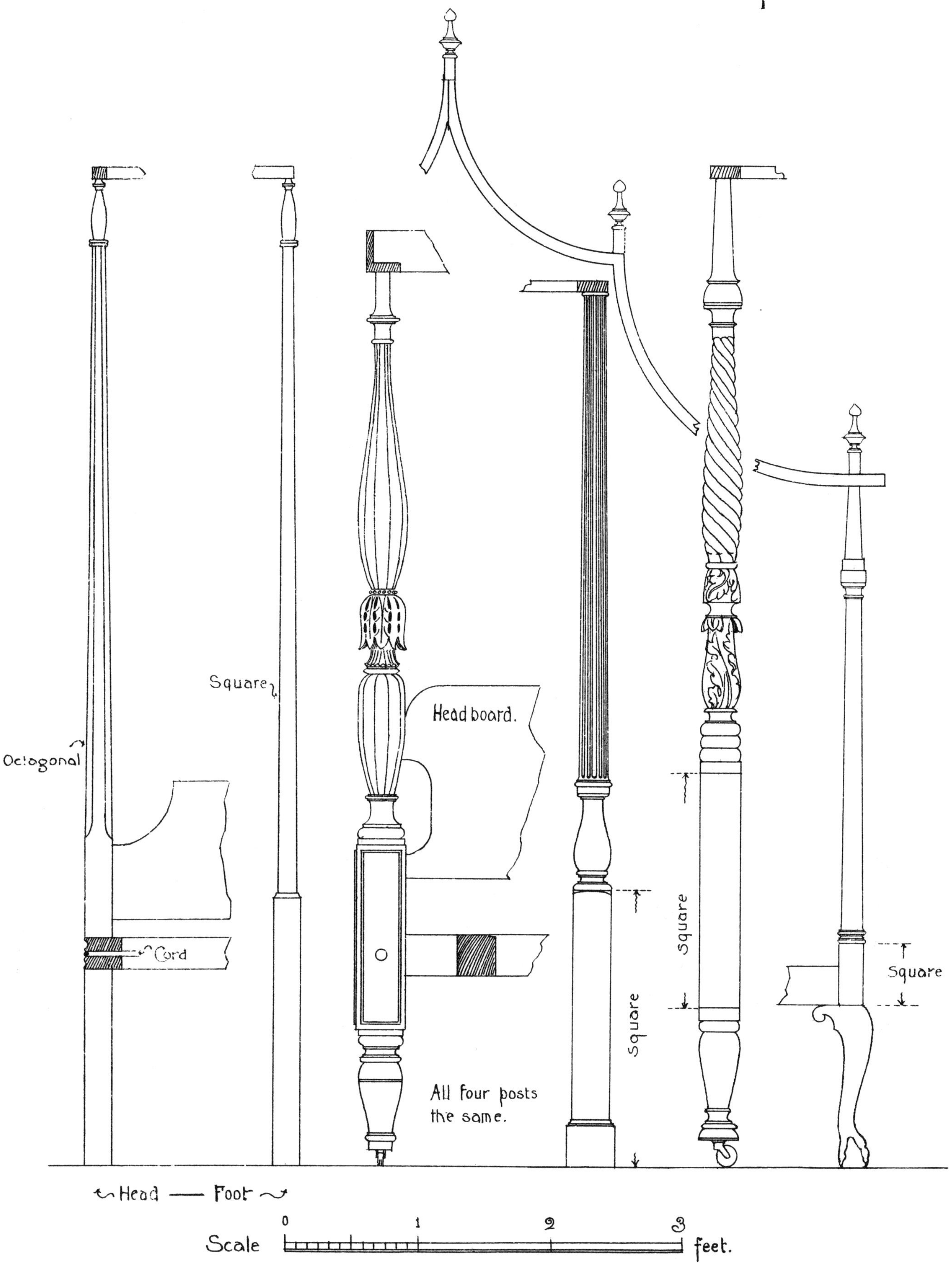

Octagonal

Square

Cord

Head board.

All four posts
the same.

Square

Square

Square

~ Head —— Foot ~

Scale | 0   1   2   3 feet.

Looking-glafs.

Frame gilded.

Socket for candle
bracket.

Scale ⊢━━━━━━━━━━━━━━━━━━┤ feet.
0   1   2   3

Looking-glaffes.

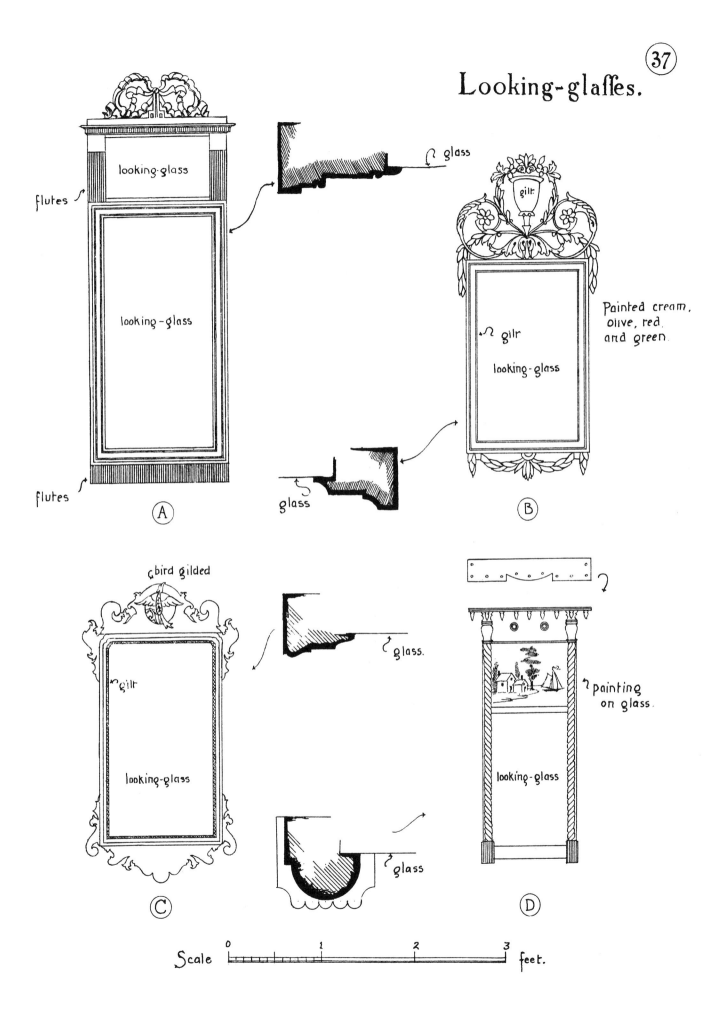

looking-glass

flutes

looking-glass

flutes

glass

glass

Ⓐ

gilt

gilt

looking-glass

Painted cream,
olive, red,
and green.

Ⓑ

bird gilded

gilt

looking-glass

glass.

glass

Ⓒ

painting
on glass.

looking-glass

Ⓓ

Scale ⊢————————————⊣ feet.
0   1   2   3

Scrutoir.
Desk.

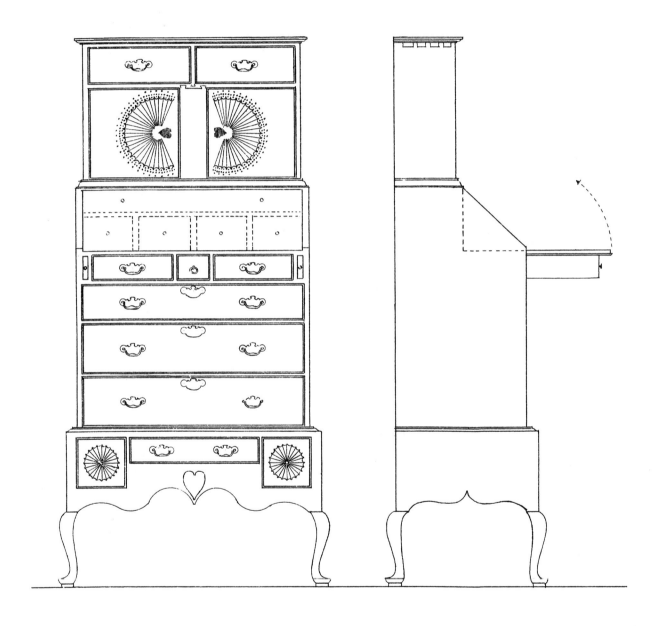

Scale |_____| feet.
0   1   2   3

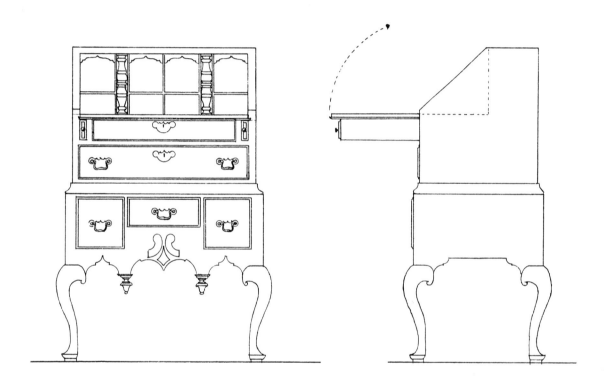

Scrutoir.
Desk.

39

Scale ⊢———————————⊣ feet.

0   1   2   3

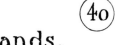

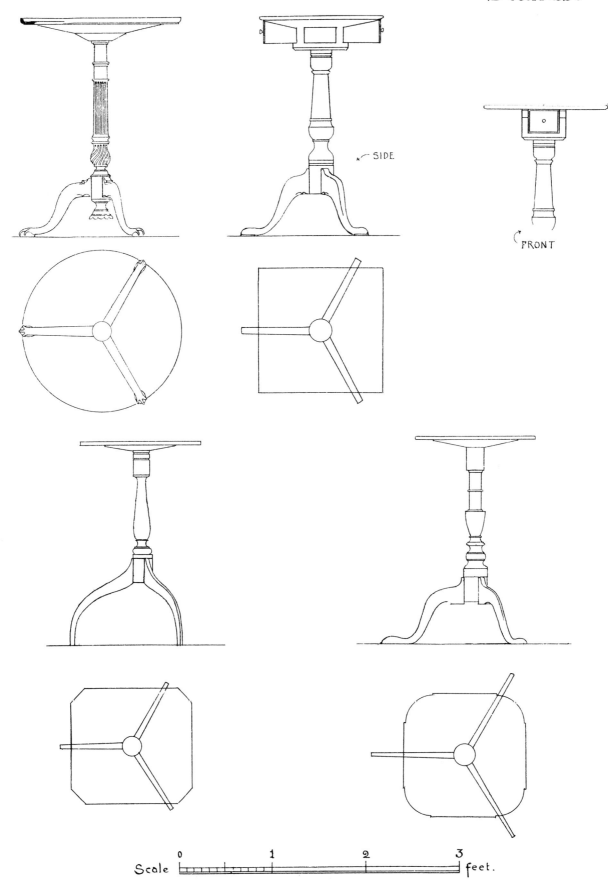

SIDE

FRONT

Scale |0 1 2 3| feet.

Feet of the Stands
shown on sheet number 40

Plan.

Plan.

Plan

Plan.

Scale 0 1 2 3 inches.

Details of Stands
shown on sheet number 40

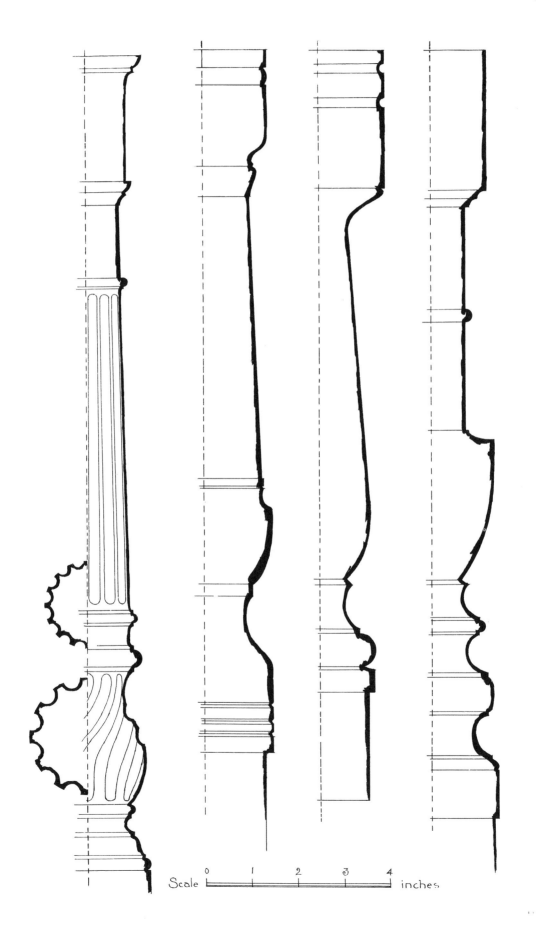

Scale 0   1   2   3   4   inches

Oval Table. (43)

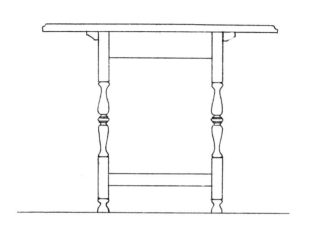

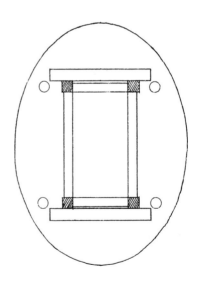

Scale 0   1   2   3   feet.

Table with leaves.

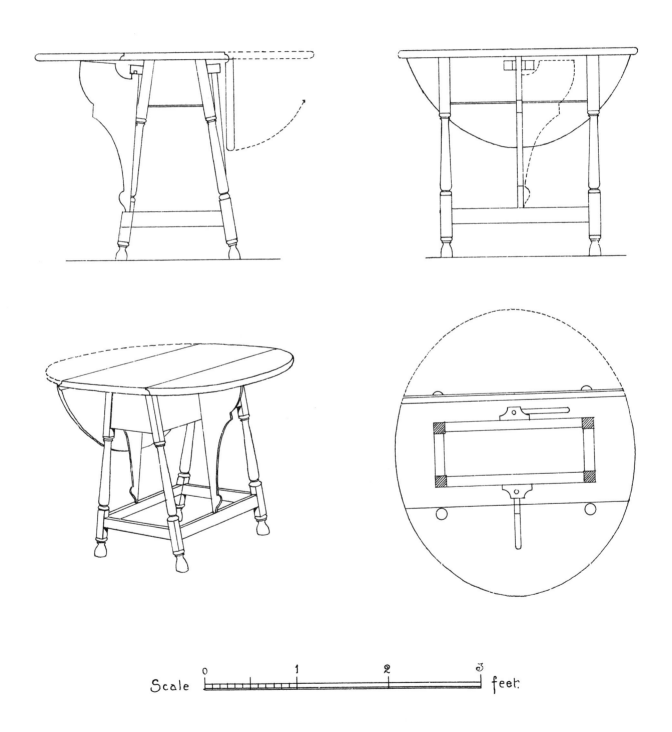

Scale   0   1   2   3   feet.

Table with leaves.

"Thousand-legged table."

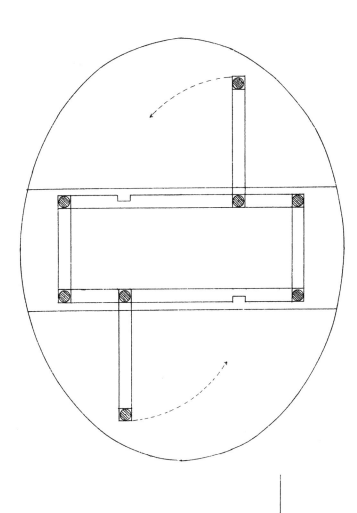

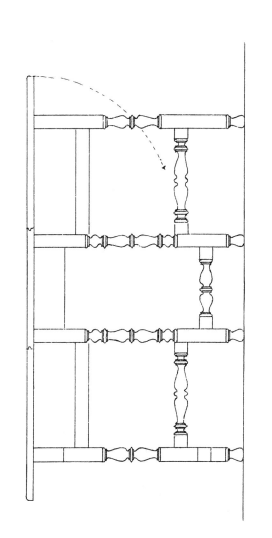

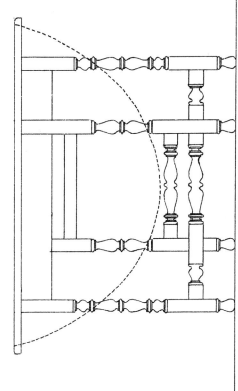

Scale   0   1   2   3 feet.

Table with leaf. (46)

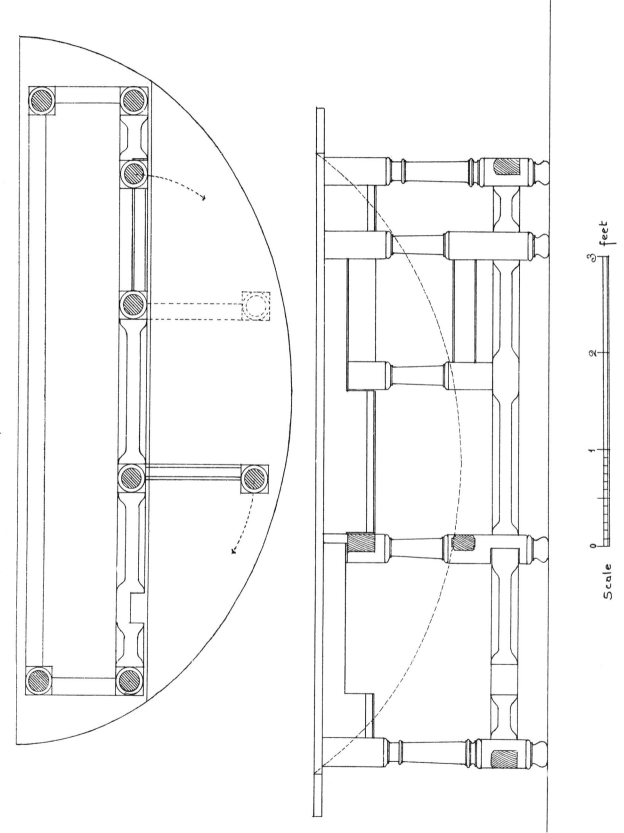

In the rooms of the Connecticut Historical Society. Hartford, Conn.

Scale

0 1 2 3 feet

Table with leaves.

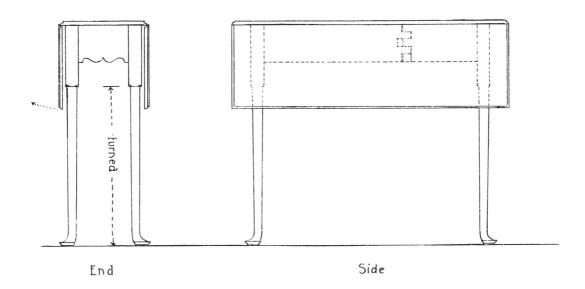

turned

End   Side

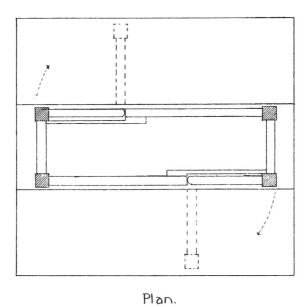

Plan.

Scale   0   1   2   3   feet.

Tea Table.

A brass rail formerly
on the edge of the top, is missing.

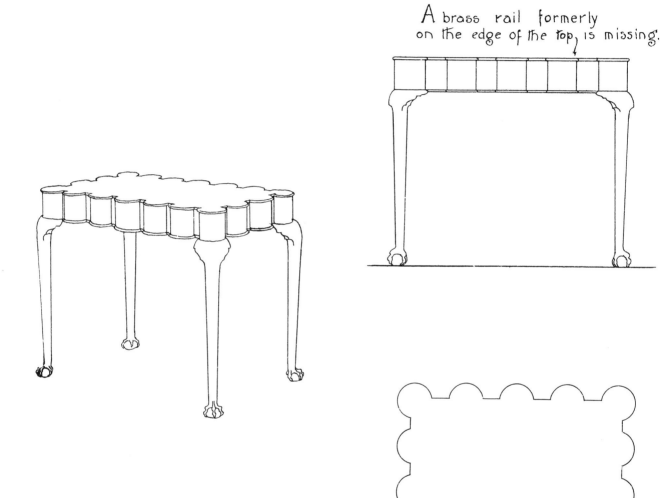

Scale [0 1 2 3] feet

Dreffing table.

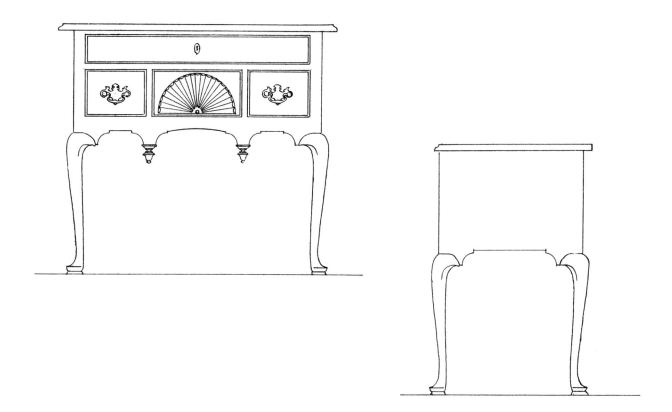

Scale  feet

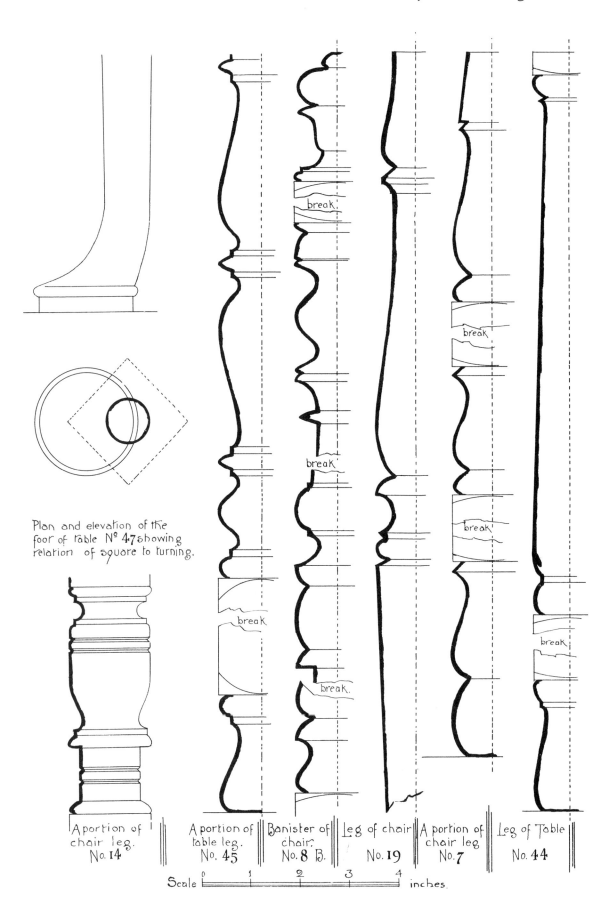

Plan and elevation of the foot of table Nº 47 showing relation of square to turning.

A portion of chair leg. No. 14   A portion of table leg. No. 45   Banister of chair. No. 8 B.   Leg of chair No. 19   A portion of chair leg No. 7   Leg of Table No. 44

Scale 0 1 2 3 4 inches.

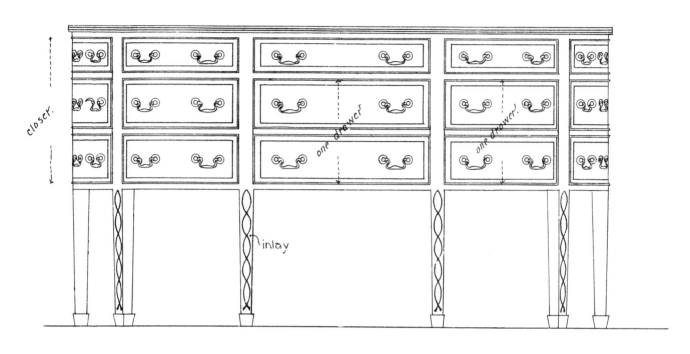

closer.

inlay

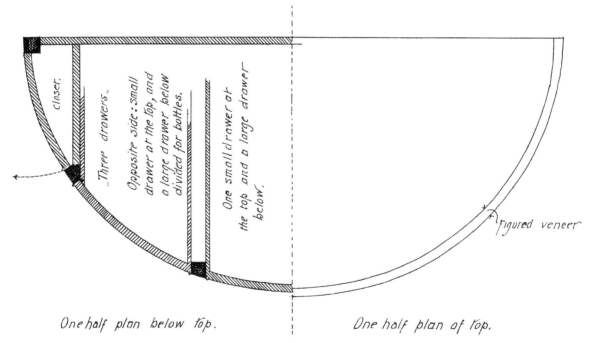

closer.

.. Three drawers.,

Opposite side : small drawer at the top, and a large drawer below, divided for bottles.

One small drawer at the top, and a large drawer below.

figured veneer

One half plan below top.

One half plan of top.

Scale 0 1 2 3 feet.

Sideboard.

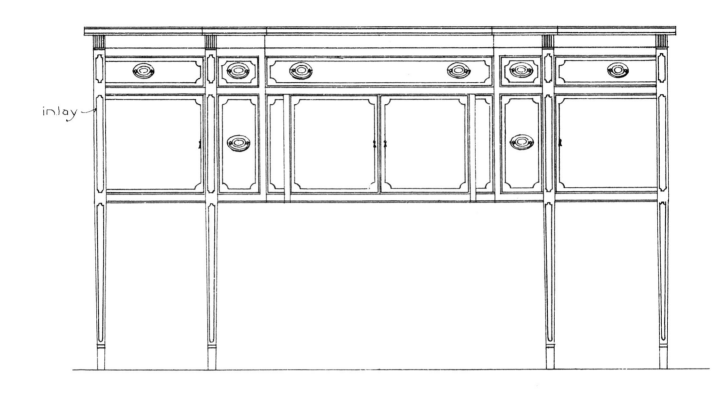

inlay

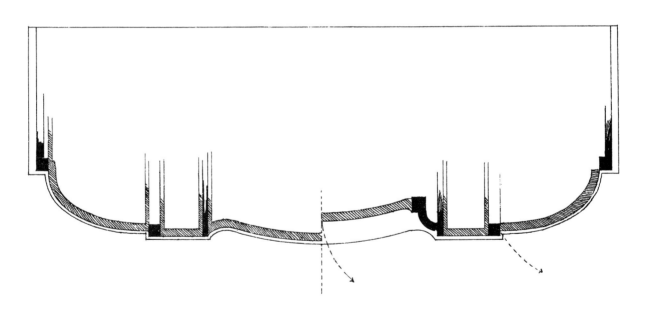

Scale   0   1   2   3   feet.

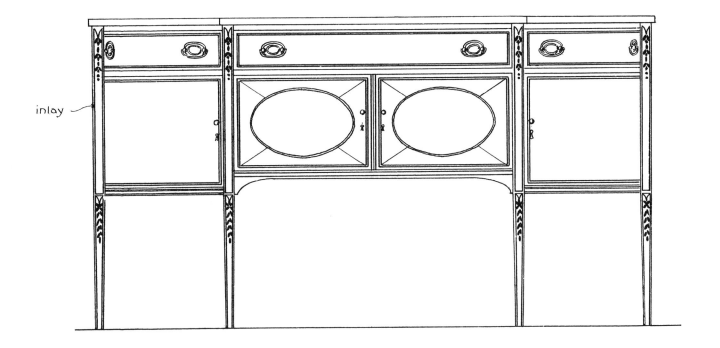

inlay

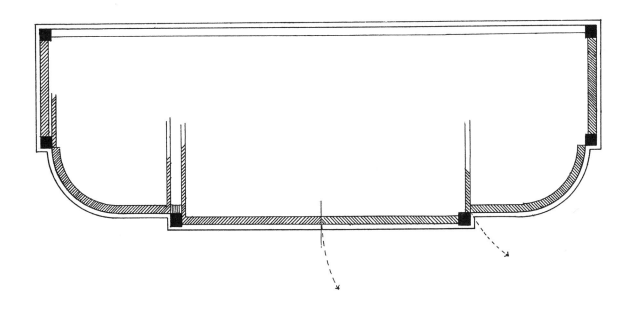

Scale | 0   1   2   3 | feet

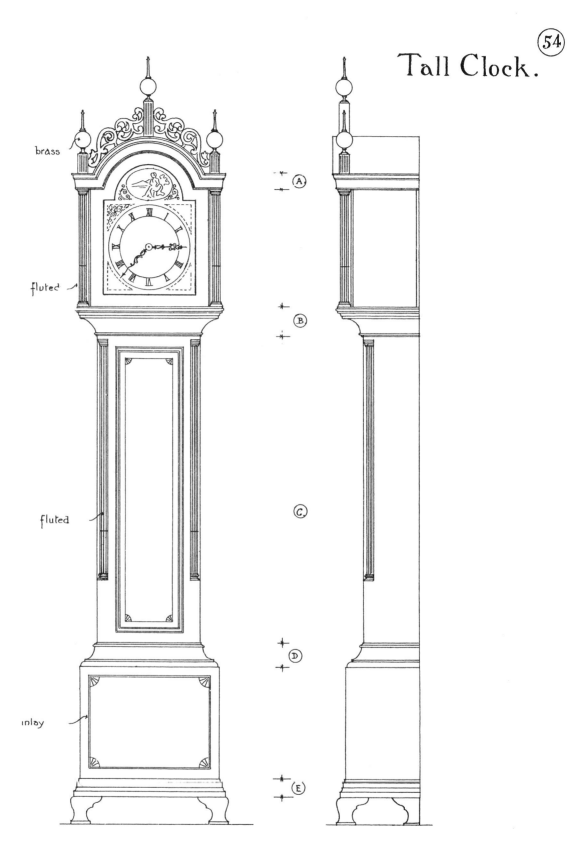

brass

fluted

fluted

inlay

Ⓐ

Ⓑ

Ⓒ

Ⓓ

Ⓔ

The sawed scroll work on
the top of the clock is a recent
restoration from memory.

Scale
0   1   2   3   feet.

Details of Tall Clock
shown on sheet № 54

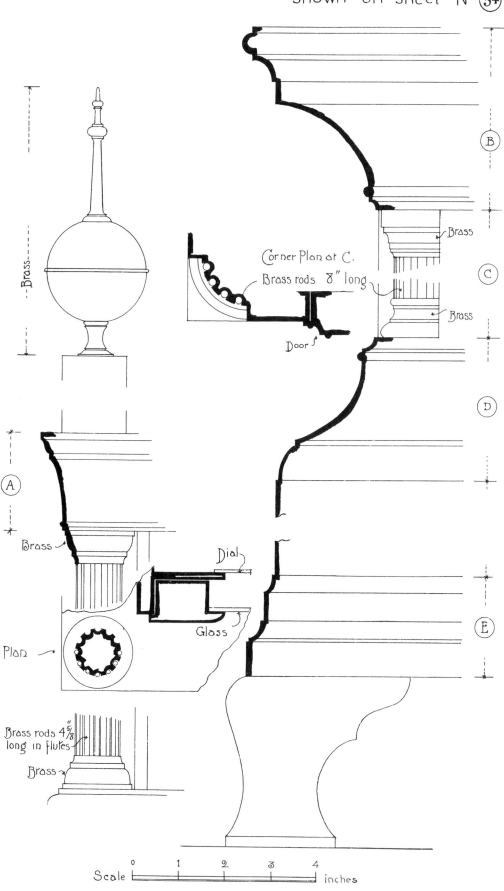

B

Brass

Corner Plan at C.
Brass rods 8″ long

C

Brass

Door

A

D

Brass

Dial

Glass

E

Plan

Brass rods 4⅝″
long in flutes

Brass

Scale |—————————————| inches
0   1   2   3   4